Latest Obsessions

KP

Made with ❤ on the BookLeaf Publishing Platform
www.bookleafpub.in
www.bookleafpub.com

Dedication

to me, to you, and the thoughts in between

Preface

these poems do not aim to define love. may you find
yourself here, in the spaces between words, and in the
echoes of your own heart

Acknowledgements

you

1. everything before the but doesn't matter

i love you but your thoughts concern me
i love you but you make me sad
i love you but you don't care
i love you but i am not the one
i love you but you lie
i love you but i don't want to talk to you
i love you but you don't see me
i love you but i don't recognize you
i love you but i want everything right now
i love but i want to stop wanting
i love you but i hate how you make me feel
i love you but i don't believe you
i love you but i hate the pain
i love you but i hate being obsessed
i love you but you don't choose me
i love you but i can't
i love you but

2. i believe you

i believe you can do anything
i believe you can do anything because
i believe you can do anything because i
i believe you can do anything because i have
i believe you can do anything because i have already
i believe you can do anything because i have already
seen
i believe you can do anything because i have already
seen you
i believe you can do anything because i have already
seen you do
i believe you can do anything because i have already
seen you do everything

3. mind melt

worrying = worshipping the problem
worrying = sad
worrying = amplifications
worrying = your mind is a liar
worrying = i am afraid
worrying = i don't trust myself
worrying = i don't trust you
worrying = i can't stop
worrying = a different story
worrying = something different
worrying = an alternate reality

4. it will be ok

it will be ok, it will be different
it will be ok, it is ok to be sad
it will be ok, you don't have to worry
it will be ok, you can be happy when you feel it
it will be ok, you will think about it a lot
it will be ok, don't spiral
it will be ok, trust yourself
it will be ok, trust the universe
it will be ok, good things happen everyday
it will be ok, even when it isn't

5. im sorry

im sorry for your confusion
im sorry for your thoughts
im sorry for your lack of communication
im sorry you lied
im sorry you can't
im sorry you don't
im sorry you won't
im sorry you cant face me
im sorry you are guilty
im sorry you are ashamed
im sorry you are gone
im sorry you are you

6. you inspire me

you inspire me to do more
you inspire me to post
you inspire me to record
you inspire me to document
you inspire me to watch
you inspire me to be me
you inspire me to try
you inspire to me see it differently
you inspire me to love me
you inspire me to love you
you inspire me to dream
you inspire me to want more
you inspire me to need more
you inspire me to see myself

7. loving you

loving you felt like loving me
more than before
more than now
more than ever

8. patterns

patterns = getting scared

patterns = running away

patterns = withdrawal

patterns = loyalty

patterns = consistency

patterns = availability

patterns = amounts

patterns = behavior

patterns = love

patterns = self love

patterns = abandonment

patterns = thoughts

patterns = spiral

9. im tired of reading your horoscope

im tired of reading your horoscope
im tired of reading your horoscope and im not in it
im tired of reading your horoscope
astrology isn't real

10. dear fear

dear fear, i am scared you don't love me

dear fear, i am scared you still think about her

dear fear, i am scared i am not the one

dear fear, i am scared you really see me

dear fear, i am scared you don't see me at all

dear fear, i am scared you will leave

dear fear, i am scared i will never get over you

dear fear, i am scared to let go

dear fear, i am scared of the future

dear fear, i am always afraid of something

dear fear, you are always there

dear fear, why don't you ever leave

dear fear, i don't fuck with you

dear fear, i hate i entertain you

dear fear, i am scared i will always be sad

dear fear, i am scared i will never be enough

dear fear, i am scared it will keep happening

dear fear, you are trash

dear fear, you try to keep me safe

dear fear, you always come true

dear fear, i will never beat you so i will do it scared

11. faith

faith does not = proof
once you have proof it is no longer faith
what if it all works out?

12. broken <3

there is nothing more whole than a broken heart
there is nothing more whole than tears that won't stop
there is nothing more whole than feeling empty
there is nothing more whole than being afraid
there is nothing more whole than self doubt
there is nothing more whole than whoever you are
where ever you are

13. projections

can you see past your projections?
how do you know what actually is?
what is truth?
where do you find the courage?
can you ever have true connection?
what is radical presence?
do you ever not see anything through the lens of an old
wound?
are all our hopeful dreams projections on different
partners?
what happens when it feels too familiar?
are our relationships with people actually relationships
with stories instead?
do we ever meet anyone where they are?
are the past disappointments, unmet needs, over
optimistic fantasies, or lingering fears all we see?
by projecting do i have control or the illusion of it?
does predicting = preventing?
if we are always predicting, are we blinded to the
present?
do we reduce others to patterns?
how do you notice the story?
can you ever let the person in front of you surprise you?

14. connections

connection lives in the moments created when we stop telling stories

15. the real you

unique
different
complicated
free
wild
unchartered
fragile
safe
real
beautiful
shining

16. action

action relieves anxiety
action relieves anxiety
action relieves anxiety

17. contrast

love starts when fear comes up

love starts when we are reminded of the past

love starts when our wires get tripped

love starts when dynamics show up

love starts when attachment styles are different

love starts when love languages aren't being heard

love starts when there is contrast

love starts when you choose it

18. yours and mine

i can't read your mind
you can't read mine

19. self

if i can ruin it before you do
we never had a chance

20. manifest

you can't manifest without the work
you can't manifest without time
you can't manifest without change
you can't manifest without self reflection
you can't manifest without growth
you can't manifest without vision
you can't manifest without help
you can't manifest without your heart

www.ingramcontent.com/pod-product-compliance
Lightning Source LLC
LaVergne TN
LVHW050249200726